A CURMUDGEON'S COMMENTARY ON THE BOOK OF REVELATION

REV. DR. RICHARD E. KUYKENDALL

This book is dedicated to
Aage Rendalen

Order this book online at www.trafford.com
or email orders@trafford.com

Most Trafford titles are also available at major online book retailers.

Printed in the United States of America.

ISBN: 978-1-4669-9667-0 (sc)
ISBN: 978-1-4669-9666-3 (e)

Trafford rev. 06/06/2013

 www.trafford.com

North America & international
toll-free: 1 888 232 4444 (USA & Canada)
fax: 812 355 4082

To my disappointments, who have ever been my most faithful teachers.

CONTENTS

INTRODUCTION

INTRODUCTION

What we are about to do here is something very unique. And that is interpret the book of Revelation, or as it is sometimes called, "The Apocalypse"—from the perspective of a cranky old curmudgeon who is sick of what everyone else has had to say about it. I am dumping previous interpretations—though we will look at some of them from time to time. And I will even argue with the book itself and what it teaches about God and "the lamb of God." But before we attempt such an unorthodox approach let me first share with you what led me to take such a course.

Traditionally, when it comes to interpreting the book of Revelation, one usually subscribes to one of the following schools of interpretation:

1. Preterist.

The Preterist school approaches the book of Revelation in terms of what was happening in the

first century. In other words, those who approach
the book in this way often believe that the book of
Revelation was written by one who believed that he
was living in the times described in the book. Thus
for these, the "beast" spoken of in chapter 13 was
the Roman Emperor or Empire which was warring
against the early church—who in turn believed
that Christ would "come quickly"[1]—that meant
within their lifetime, destroy the beast power in the
apocalyptic battle of Armageddon and thus establish
a millennial reign of peace.

Thus the book is not seen as a futuristic prophecy
of the end of the world but rather as an apocalyptic
description of what was happening to the early
Christians and what they believed God was going to
do about it.

2. Futurist.

The Futurist school approaches the book of
Revelation in such a way that, with the exception
of the "letters to the seven churches,"[2] the book is
a description of what will happen at the end of the
world. In other words, those who approach the book
in this way often believe that the book of Revelation
was written by one who was in effect only a

---

[1]   Revelation 22:7, 12, 20
[2]   See chapters 2-3

"mouthpiece" through whom God spoke concerning those events which would transpire in the time of the end. Therefore, the book was a "sealed book" to those of the first century. And though it had some application to the events which were taking place at the time of its writing, the true meaning would not be known or take place until "the last days." Thus for these the beast is the "antichrist" who is yet to come and who will attempt to deceive the world into following his rule rather than that of Christ's. And the battle of Armageddon is therefore yet to come and is often described as what in effect would be World War III. Thus the book is seen as a futuristic prophecy of the time of the end.

3. Historicist.

The Historicist school approaches the book of Revelation in terms of an unfolding of events beginning in the first century and climaxing in the creation of "a new heaven and a new earth."[3] In other words, those who approach the book in this way often believe that the various series of sevens—such as the seven churches, seals, trumpets, and plagues—describe history in advance—from the author's present and through to the end of the world as we know it. Therefore in each sequence of seven,

---

[3]   Revelation 21:1

one would be a description of what was transpiring in the first century while seven would be a description of what will happen at the consummation of all things. Accordingly, two through six would describe the time between one and seven. Thus for these the beast, as well as the last in each series of seven is often seen in terms much the same as the futurist while the first in each series of seven is seen in terms similar to the preterist's interpretation. Thus the book is seen as a historical unfolding of time from the early church to the new earth.

4. Symbolic.

Most of these approach the book of Revelation in purely symbolic terms—often believing that there is an esoteric or allegorical meaning to the book which is independent of any specific time frame. These often feel that the author of the book was not portraying any particular external event in history but rather describing certain spiritual truths in symbolic language which only those "who have ears to hear and eyes to see" are able to understand. Thus for these the beast or any other symbol in the book can be interpreted in any number of ways depending on the particular school of interpretation.[4]

---

[4] For example see Edgar Cayce's *A Commentary on the book of Revelation*. A. R. E. Press, Virginia, 1988.

The problem with all of the above mentioned interpretations for the layperson is: How does one know which one is the right one? For often these interpretations not only contradict one another but at times even say completely opposite things. For instance, some historicists interpret the rider on the while horse in the seven seals (6:2) to be the early church in its Christ-like purity—imitating their Lord as described in chapter 19. While some preterists identify the same rider as the antichrist—impersonating the true Christ portrayed in chapter 19. While according to Edgar Cayce, the white horse is symbolic of the human gonads.[5]

Most often laypeople simply accept the particular interpretation which is held by their denomination (if there is a denominational position) or by their minister. And where a certain interpretation does not seem to fit well—most simply concede that it is beyond their ability to understand. Some even get to the point where they feel that the book is either unintelligible or plain nonsense that none could ever hope to understand[6]—though many think they do.

Having studied this book at both the undergraduate and graduate levels, and having

---

[5] Ibid. pp. 90-91.
[6] See: D. H. Lawrence, *Apocalypse*, pp. 7-11. The Viking Press, New York.

written a major paper while in seminary on the book[7] I am well aware of these problems. And these problems have become even more apparent since my days in seminary as I have taught seminar classes on the book of Revelation.

So why try approaching the book from yet another angle? Will this not just muddy the water even more than it already is? I think not—for sometimes it is helpful to step back from something which seems beyond our ability to deal with and then come at it again from another angle. Doing this sometimes gives us a fresh perspective on things. And this is what I am attempting to do here.

Having taught the book of Revelation from both a verse by verse approach as well as from a topical approach, and having taught it from the preterist, futurist, historicist and symbolic perspectives, I am well aware of the inherent difficulties in each of these—especially when you are attempting to be true to the author's original intent do you confront enormous problems. Depending on your presuppositions concerning the concept of "divine inspiration" you could see the book as composed of divinely inspired prophecies of the future or esoteric truths uttered for the sake of "the elect" and then interpret the book accordingly—feeling that you

---

[7]   "The Theological Use of Time in the Apocalypse."

were being true to the author's intent. If however you did not accept the idea of "divine inspiration" as traditionally understood, you would probably interpret the book in view of the situation in the first century and consider it a purely human construction.

The problem with any of the afore mentioned positions is that they are dependent upon the beliefs of the interpreter and thus cannot be evaluated objectively.

What I am attempting to do in this book is to side-step all of these issues—for in this book I am not going to proceed on the assumption that I know what the author's original intent was. In fact, here it is not even essential that we know what the author intended, for we are going to attempt to see what the book can say to us as individuals rather than what it was supposed to have said to the author's original audience or to any other supposed audience throughout history.

It is my hope that in this book you will be able to look at the Apocalypse in a fresh new way and see it as having more than simply prophetic content. Perhaps by the time you finish this book you will find that you don't looks at things the way you used to look at them . . .

CHAPTER 1

Four Kinds of Symbols

FOUR KINDS OF SYMBOLS

Before we begin our study of the book of Revelation I felt that it would be helpful to first distinguish between four different kinds of symbols. This will aid us in our interpretation of the sometimes bizarre imagery we are confronted with in the book of Revelation.

First of all however, what do we mean when we use the word "symbol"? When we turn to a dictionary in order to find out how the word "symbol" is defined we discover that there are a number of definitions. In this book however, we will be working with reference to the following definition:

> "something that stands for or suggests something else by reason of relationship, association, convention, or accidental resemblance; esp: a visible

sign of something invisible (the lion is a symbol of courage.)"[8]

Thus having stated our working definition, let us now look at four different kinds of symbols.

1. National and Secular Symbols.

Examples of these kinds of symbols are often very obvious. From the flags of different nations to those symbols which act as visual representations of the guiding philosophies of certain nations, such as the Soviet Union's hammer and sickle, or which represent in a purely abstract form the dominant ideology of a particular nation, such as Nazi Germany's swastika.

Besides these, there are other kinds of national symbols which were not created as such but which have become such with time, such as New York's "Statue of Liberty" or Paris' "Eiffel Tower." And then there are the various animal symbols, such as America's eagle or China's dragon. And in the American political arena we have the Democrat's donkey and the Republican's elephant.

---

[8] *Webster's Ninth New Collegiate*, p. 1195. Merriam-Webster Inc., Publishers. Massachusetts. 1988.

The above merely hints at the various kinds of national symbols. And, beyond these there are numerous secular symbols which are used within a nation. From restroom facility markers to road signs to symbols used as logos for various businesses and organizations. In all of these instances the appearance of any one of these symbols brings to mind the concept or even a whole ideology behind that for which the symbol stands and thus it functions in a way similar to shorthand.

2. Religious Symbols.

Examples of these kinds of symbols are easily recognizable. From those symbols which act as visual representations of the guiding philosophies of certain world religions, such as Christianity's cross or Taoism's "yin and Yang", to those symbols which abstractly represent the religion, such as Judaism's Star of David.

Besides these, there are other kinds of religious symbols which are utilized in various rituals, such as the Eucharistic elements used in Christianity's reenactment of Christ's Last Supper.

Beyond this, many religions even possess certain "graven images" which symbolize various deities or divine beings. Again, in all of these instances the appearance of any one of these symbols brings to mind those ideas for which the symbol stands and thus acts as a kind of religious shorthand.

3. Personal Symbols.

Examples of what I refer to as "personal symbols" differ from one individual to another and thus hold purely subjective meanings. The meaning of personal symbols, though in most cases emotionally powerful, operate at a subconscious level and may oftentimes not be consciously recognized. Through self-reflection however one can begin to understand which characters, objects and situations act as personal symbols in one's life.

For instance, my daughter some time ago had a dream that she had gone to Sunday School and found a refrigerator in the class room. In talking with her I found that she had only positive associations with refrigerators—seeing them as a place where she could get food. With this in mind I told her that the appearance of a refrigerator in her Sunday School room in this dream would suggest that she saw her Sunday School as a place where she could partake of "spiritual food"—"food for the soul."

This interpretation of the "refrigerator symbol" however is an individual interpretation based on personal associations. If for instance, my daughter had climbed into a refrigerator as a child and had become trapped, the appearance of a refrigerator in her Sunday School room in a dream would have instead functioned as an object of fear, suggesting more than likely that she felt trapped or suffocated in Sunday School.

And besides objects such as refrigerators—personal symbols can also be formed through various associations with animals, certain people, places and situations. Thus the content of any meaningful, intense or exceptional experience can become an acquisition into the individual's library of symbols—each symbol in turn standing for a certain emotional association and thus acting as a kind of emotional shorthand.

4. Archetypal or Universal Symbols.

Since the time of the Swiss psychologist, Carl Gustav Jung (1875-1961)—psychologists, students of mythology and others have seen that there are certain symbols which are common to the entire race. These symbols appear in myths, legends, fairy tales and old stories as well as in dreams. Because certain characters, themes and images recur throughout the thought and feeling life of all cultures, these are considered to be archetypal or universal symbols.

Examples of these kinds of symbols on the "dark side" would be the various monsters and demons which portray our inner fears and the stranger who most often depicts the dark or hidden side of ourselves. These symbols often warn us of the need to deal with certain issues in our lives. While on the positive side, the wise old man, the magical child or the eternal mother suggest various nurturing themes.

Then there are certain activities in our dreams such as flying which suggest transcending difficulties or sexual union—suggesting integration of certain qualities. While fleeing or falling often suggests avoidance of certain problems or feelings of victimization. And there are also other kinds of symbols such as the tree which symbolizes growth, the rainbow which represents hope or promise, or the dove which represents peace.

Of course these are only generalizations for when we are dealing with any of these symbols we must always take into consideration any personal associations with the image, the mood or feeling which is conveyed by the image and the situation under which the image came to the person. For instance, for a child, the appearance of a bear in a dream (here acting as a kind of archetypal monster) would in most cases function as an expression or embodiment of certain inner fears, while for a zoologist who had been unsuccessful in tracking a bear for a certain study—the appearance of a bear in a dream would more than likely be an expression of wish fulfillment. Thus, though these symbols have archetypal and universal meanings, we must always consider them within the total context of the circumstances of their origin.

This then leads us to how we will apply these distinctions concerning the symbols to the imagery we encounter in the book of Revelation.

In considering any passage, though we may assume that all symbols are religious in that they appear in a biblical text, we will still need to distinguish whether the symbol is purely a religious symbol—unique to the Judeo-Christian tradition or whether it is a universal symbol. More than this we must take into consideration the circumstances under which the passage was written in view of the author's beliefs, expectations and the author's world in general—this may in turn bring into view certain national and secular symbols.

Personal symbols in such a study would be extremely speculative due to our lack of information concerning the author's personal life.

CHAPTER 2

An Initial Answer to the Problem

AN INITIAL ANSWER TO THE PROBLEM

Though we will find that there are a number of conflicts presented in the book of Revelation, the first chapter is written from the perspective of that problem which is of central concern to the author of the book—the overriding problem being that of the persecution of the early church. Many in fact believe that the book of Revelation was written during the persecution of the Roman Emperor Domitian, and believe that John himself was in exile on the island of Patmos, a penal colony about thirty-five miles off the coast of what today is Turkey.

In the introduction, John identifies with his fellow sufferers on the mainland with the words,

> "I John, your brother, who share with you in Jesus the tribulation and the kingdom and the patient endurance, was

on the island called Patmos on account of the word of God and the testimony of Jesus."

Amidst the religious conflict of his time—his only crime being that he thought differently than those in power—his spirit rose above his physical situation and he perceived a resolution to his and his church's almost overwhelming conflict. He writes to share the hope of the resolution which he sees, with his people—the church.

And as with many of us, though he faces a central overriding conflict and longs for its resolution—this is by no means the only problem. There are a host of smaller problems which need resolution as well. And so as he proceeds we find that while the first chapter provides an initial answer for the overriding problem (which we shall consider in a moment)—the final resolution comes in full only at the conclusion of the book. Thus following the initial answer we encounter a number of other conflicts which also must be resolved.

As for the initial answer to the central problem we see the following:

1. The problem is addressed by God, "the Almighty" (1:8), and thus resolution is assured.

2. The problem is addressed more specifically in view of the life, death and resurrection of Jesus Christ.

Upon mentioning Jesus Christ, John is reminded of the fact that Jesus was a "faithful witness" and though he died as a result of that witness, he became "the first-born of the dead" (1:5). Christ himself says later in the chapter,

> "Fear not, I am the first and the last, and the living one; I died, and behold I am alive for ever more, and I have the keys of Death and Hades" (1:17b-18).

Thus this being the ultimate result of Christ's witness, John and his fellow sufferers can expect ultimate victory as well, despite the fact that present appearances seem hopeless.

More than this, John is told that Christ is the "ruler of kings on earth"(1:5)—thus though it may seem as though the Emperor is in control—things are not as they seem! And the tables will one day turn for Christ has made those who follow him "a kingdom" (1:6).

3. The problem is addressed in a symbolic way in John's first vision (1:12-20).

Though many images come together to form this majestic picture of the glorified and triumphant Christ, two of the symbols are interpreted for us in verse 20. The others are taken from the vast storehouse of Jewish religious symbols. Compare for instance verses 11-17 with parts of chapter seven and ten of the book of Daniel and one will see that these were familiar religious symbols within the Jewish tradition.

Revelation 1:11-17	Daniel 7 & 10
one like a son of man	one like a son of man (7:13)
clothed with a long robe and with a golden girdle round his breast	clothed in linen, whose loins were girded with gold of Uphaz (10:5)
his head and his hair were white as white wool, white as snow	his raiment was white as snow, and the hair of his head like pure wool (7:9)
his eyes were like a flame of fire	his eyes like flaming torches (10:6)
his feet were like burnished bronze, refined as in a furnace	his arms and legs like the gleam of burnished bronze (10:6)

his voice was like the sound of many waters	the sound of his words like the noise of a multitude (10:6)
when I saw him, I fell at his feet as though dead. But he laid his right hand upon me, saying, "Fear not . . ."	when I heard the sound of His words, I fell on my face in a deep sleep with my face to the ground. And behold, a hand touched me . . . Then he said to me, "Fear not . . ." (10:9-10, 12)

And it is not accidental that the author recalls the book of Daniel for this recollection itself brings to mind a similar conflict which seemed impossible to those of the past but which found resolution.

Considering other images in this vision we find that the "sharp two-edged sword" which issues from Christ's mouth is a symbol of the decisiveness of his word—

> "For the word of God is living and active, sharper than any two-edged sword . . ."[9]

---

[9] Hebrews 4:12. Also see Isaiah 49:2.

Though this whole picture brings an answer to the central conflict in the portrait of the triumphant Christ, the focus is on his presence in the midst of the seven golden lampstands and the seven stars which he holds in his right hand.

Though there is some similarity between the image of the seven lampstands here and the image which appears in the fourth chapter of Zechariah, John is told specifically the meaning of these lampstands. Here the lampstands represent the churches and Christ standing in the midst of them—he is not far removed—he is there with them. And though not always apparent to outward perception, he is there just the same.[10]

When we come to the image of the seven stars, John is told that they are symbolic of the angels of the seven churches. In the Greek language the word translated "angels" can also be translated "messengers"—that is any messenger of God and not simply divine beings. If this were the case the image would suggest that besides standing in the midst of the churches, Christ holds the leaders of the churches in his "right hand"—which in the Jewish culture suggested the hand of favor and strength. Long before it was sung, "He's got the whole world

---

[10] For a vivid account of this same kind of idea see: 2 Kings 6:8-17.

in his hands" it was said that he holds his messengers in his hand—John himself being such a messenger.

Thus we see, that faced with the overriding problem of the persecution of the church, John receives and in turn delivers an initial answer to the apparent triumph of earthly powers over the church—and this answer is the triumphant Christ who stands in the midst of the churches and who holds his messengers in his right hand. Thus it is Christ who is ultimately in control.

What does all of this then say to us? It tells us that in the midst of our lives stands one who is triumphant and who holds us in his hands.[11]

But some might reply that this is only an initial answer—in the meantime we continue to suffer as did the church of old—many of which did not see the resolution of that conflict within their lifetimes.

Chapter one's answer to this is "patient endurance" while one lives and in the case that one dies, the recognition that Christ himself died as well but that he now hold "the keys of Death and Hades" (1:18).

Though the first part of this answer that is the response of "patient endurance" is by no means a magical solution as in the "deus ex machina," it is better than falling prey to despair. And as for the

---

[11]   See: John 10:27-29.

second part of this answer, that is the hope in a life after death—though this belief cannot be proven to be true, it can be proven that such a belief has given hope to those in seemingly hopeless situations. It can also provide a reward for "patient endurance" and thus acts as a motivation in apparently no-win situations.

CHAPTER 3

What Kind of Person am I Anyway?

WHAT KIND OF PERSON
AM I ANYWAY?

In the next two chapters (2&3) of the book of Revelation are the letters to the seven churches.[12] The seven churches were all located in what today is Turkey. The seven cities where the churches were located form a circle.

When I came to these letters, I asked the question, "Why these seven churches?" Why not seven churches in Israel? The reason probably has to do with the fact that the Christians fled Jerusalem not long before it was destroyed by the Romans. Also we see in the book of Acts that it was clear that the Jews were not interested in embracing Jesus or his followers as part of their faith. More than this, tradition tells us that John was at the church

---

[12] As you will see, the book of Revelation has a number of series of seven, such as the seven letters to the churches, the seven seals, the seven trumpets and the seven last plagues.

in Ephesus before he was exiled to the island of Patmos. And one tradition even tells us that Mary the mother of Jesus was also there—and Ephesus is the first of the seven churches which receive a letter.

In discussing the seven letters, biblical scholars would discuss the historical background of these churches and where they were located in relationship to their place in the Roman Empire. And they also look at their unique features in terms of what is written in the letters. I on the other hand am not writing as a biblical scholar or commentator. Rather I am looking at the letters in terms of what they can teach us about ourselves.

The first thing I do when I look at the seven letters is I see them as revealing seven personality types. So the question arises in light of this, "What kind of person am I anyway?"—in relation to the seven churches? Let's look at each of them, and then, you the reader, try to identify which church describes you best.

The Seven Letters to the Seven Churches.

The first thing I will mention as we look at these seven letters—which are actually addressed to "the angel" of each church, is that each letter follows the same pattern. As I said, first they say that the letter is addressed to the angel of the church then they say

"These are the words of . . ."—then the author of each letter identifies himself by a different aspect of the first vision of the triumphant Christ—for instance in the first letter the author identifies himself as "him who holds the seven stars in his right hand, who walks among the seven golden lampstands."

Next the letters say something that Christ knows about their church. Then they are given counsel. Each letter then ends with the words, "Let those who have ears, hear what the Spirit is saying to the churches" and those who "overcome" in each church are given their own unique promise.

The first letter to the churches as I mentioned above is the letter "to the angel of the church in Ephesus" (2:1-7). The letter identifies the author as "he who holds the seven stars in his right hand, and who walks in the midst of the seven golden candlesticks." In saying this he is showing the church that he holds them in his hand, and he is with them—even though it may not seem so.

Then he points out there is good news, and bad news. The good news is that he knows they are enduring patiently, that they do not put up with evil, and that they have labored for his name's sake. The bad news is that they have left their first love—somehow though they are laboring for him, and not putting up with evil, they are not working out of love. It's like they are in a loveless marriage. They can get along with each other like roommates, and they can do what needs to be done, but they are no longer in love. Jesus tells them that they need to recapture that love they had in the beginning. Another comparison is how the Pharisees are depicted in the gospels. They keep the law, they do their rituals, they do not put up with evil, but they are not doing these things out of love.

He then warns them that if they do not recapture that love he will remove their candlestick—and you know what that means—probably no heaven for you! Are you working out of love or just doing what you have to do?

The second letter to the churches is the letter "to the angel of the church in Smyrna" (2:8-11). The letter identifies the author as "the first and the last, who was dead, and is alive." In saying this he is showing the church that though they may have to die, yet there will be life after death.

Then he points out that he knows they are afflicted and poor, and how others slander them. Then he tells them not to fear what they are going to suffer—some may go to prison, and some may die, but they must be faithful unto death if they would wear the crown of life. His promise to them is that if they overcome they will not be hurt by the "second death." The second death is the death in which there is no resurrection. We will look at this when we get to chapter 20 of the Apocalypse.

The third letter to the churches is the letter "to the angel of the church in Pergamum" (2:12-17). The letter identifies the author as "him who has the sharp two-edged sword." In saying this he is he is revealing himself as the one who speaks the word of God.

Then he points out there is good news, and bad news. The good news is that they are holding fast to his name even while living where "Satan's throne is"—for us this could mean doing good even when you're in a bad environment. The bad news however is that they are eating food that had been sacrificed to idols, and committing fornication. For us this could mean eating and drinking addictions and sexual immorality—I'll let you decide what is immoral and what is not.

He then warns them that if they don't change in view of their addictions he will judge them with the sword of his mouth—or in view of "God's word." His promise to them is that if they overcome they will receive manna—the food of God, and they will also receive a white stone with their new name on it. A white stone means judgment in your favor and a new name means a new you!

The fourth letter to the churches is the letter "to the angel of the church in Thyatira" (2:18-29). The letter identifies the author as "the Son of God, who has eyes like a flame of fire, and whose feet are like burnished bronze." In saying this he is saying that he sees what you're doing or as it says later in this letter, he is "the one who searches minds and hearts," and he "will give to each of you as your works deserve." I once had a theology professor who said that one's true character is revealed in what you would do if you knew no one would see you do it. And having feet of bronze, if he were to walk on you, you would die.

Then again he points out there is good news, and bad news. The good news is that he knows of their love, faith, service, and patient endurance—that's real good! The bad news however is that they are tolerating evil in their midst—allowing some to teach that it is okay to eat what they shouldn't and to practice sexual immorality. Again, I'll let you be the judge of what is immoral and what is not.

He then warns them that if they don't change he will give them what their works deserve—that too is what the law of karma teaches—"what you sew, that shall you reap" or "what goes around comes around!" His promise to them on the other hand is that if they overcome he will give them authority over others, and "the morning star" which is Christ himself as we find out in 22:16.

The fifth letter to the churches is the letter "to the angel of the church in Sardis" (3:1-6). The letter identifies the author as "him who has the seven spirits of God and the seven stars." In saying this he is saying that he is filled with the fullness of the Spirit—seven being complete in the book of Revelation. And he holds them in his hand, as in "He's got the whole world in his hands . . ."

In this letter he says that he knows their works—that they have a name of being alive, but they are dead—they are the living dead! He then warns them that if they don't change he will come to them in an hour that they don't know. And as they are figuratively dead now, when he comes they will be really dead. His promise to them is that if they overcome they will be clothed in white raiment—that is they will be seen as pure, and he will not blot their names out of the book of life, but rather he will confess their names to God.

The sixth letter to the churches is the letter "to the angel of the church in Philadelphia" (3:7-13). The letter identifies the author as "the holy one, the true one, who has the key of David, who opens and no one shuts, who shuts and no one opens." In saying this he is pointing out that he is the one who opens doors and closes doors in our lives.

As in the letter to the angel of Smyrna, this letter has no bad news in terms of their behavior. Rather he says that he knows their works—how they have kept his word of patient endurance and not denied him. He says that one day he will have their enemies bow down before them.

In this letter there are no words of warning. Rather, his promise to them is that if they overcome he will make them "pillars" in the temple of God—as in "he's a pillar in the community." More than this he will write on them the name of God, the New Jerusalem, and his own new name—in other words, "You'll be in!"

The seventh and final letter to the churches is the letter "to the angel of the church in Laodicea" (3:14-22). The letter identifies the author as "the Amen, the faithful and true witness, the beginning of God's creation." In saying this he is saying that he is the beginning and the end.

Then he says he knows their works—that they are neither hot nor cold, rather they are lukewarm, and he is about to spit them out of his mouth. He says that though they say they are rich and in need of nothing—that is physically—they don't realize that they are wretched, miserable, poor, blind and naked.

His promise to them is that if they overcome they will sit with him on his throne.

The seventh letter also has these famous words: "Behold I stand at the door and knock. If anyone hears my voice and opens the door, I will come in and sup with him, and he with me."

So, which church do you identify with the most? What kind of person are you anyway?

CHAPTER 4

A Vision of Heaven

A VISION OF HEAVEN

In chapters 4-5 John has a vision of Heaven. As it says in the first verse of chapter four, "After this I looked, and there in heaven was an opened door."

John sees a number of things there. First he sees the throne of God with an emerald rainbow around it. Around the throne there are twenty-four thrones with twenty-four elders sitting upon them—I see them as the twelve patriarchs of the twelve tribes of Israel, and the twelve apostles. Then John sees "four living creatures." Below is a description of the four living creatures and their parallels in Isaiah 6 and Ezekiel 1.

Revelation 4:6-8	Isaiah 6 & Ezekiel 1
And round the throne, on each side of the throne, are four living creatures	And from the midst of it came the likeness of four living creatures (Eze. 1:5)

the first living creature like a lion	the four had the face of a lion on the right side (Eze. 1:10)
the second living creature like an ox	the four had the face of an ox on the left side (Eze. 1:10)
the third living creature with the face of a man	each had the face of a man in the front (Eze. 1:10)
the fourth living creature like a flying eagle	the four had the face of an eagle at the back (Eze. 1:10)
And the four living creatures, each of them with six wings	the seraphim; each had six wings (Isa.6:2)[13]
are full of eyes all round and within	their rims were full of eyes round about (Eze. 1:18)[14]

---

[13] The living creatures in Ezekiel have four wings (1:6).

[14] Note the eyes in Ezekiel's account appear on the rim of "Ezekiel's wheels."

and day and night they never cease to sing, "Holy, holy, holy, is the Lord God Almighty . . ."	and one called to another and said, "Holy, holy, holy, is the Lord of hosts . . ." (Isa. 6:3)

John then sees that the one sitting on the throne of God (and we're assuming it is God) is holding in his right hand a scroll with seven seals on it. Then he sees an angel who proclaims with a loud voice, "Who is worthy to open the scroll and break its seals?" No one is found worthy in heaven or earth. John begins to "weep bitterly" but then one of the twenty-for elders says, "Do not weep for the Lion of the tribe of Judah, the root of David has conquered, and can open the scroll and its seals."

Then John sees a Lamb as if it had been slain, having seven horns and seven eyes—which are the seven spirits of God. The Lamb—which is Christ "the lamb of God who takes away the sins of the world" (John 1:29) takes the scroll from the hand of him who sits upon the throne. When he does this the four living creatures and the twenty-four elders sing, "You are worthy to take the scroll and open its seals . . ." Then all the angels of heaven and every creature on earth sing, "Worthy is the Lamb that was slain . . ."

CHAPTER 5

The Seven Seals

THE SEVEN SEALS

The seven seals run from chapter six to the first verse of chapter eight. Chapter seven is an interlude which we will also discuss in this chapter. I see the seven seals as parallel to Matthew 24 where Jesus speaks of "the end of the age," and his "second coming."

The first four seals that are opened are referred to as "The Four Horsemen of the Apocalypse." For us this could be the four "nightmares"—get it?— "mares." Below is a description of the four horsemen and their parallels in Zechariah 6.

Revelation 6:2-8   Zechariah 6:2-3[15]

a white horse, and its   the third white horses
rider   (verse 3)

---

[15]   Note: These go forth to the four winds to "patrol the earth." See: Zechariah 6:7. (New Revised Standard Version).

another horse, bright red; its rider	the first chariot had red horses (verse 2)
a black horse, and its rider	the second black horses (verse 2)
a pale horse, and its rider	the fourth chariot dappled gray horses (verse 3)

The Lamb opens the first seal and John sees a white horse with a rider who is wearing a crown and having a bow—as in bow and arrow. I tend to see this horseman as a false Christ as Jesus speaks of it in Matthew 24:5, 23-27. I see this horseman as a poor impersonation of Christ on the white horse in chapter 19:11-16. Both are on white horses but this horseman carries a bow and wears a crown, while Christ has a sharp sword coming out of his mouth and on his head are many diadems. For us this could speak of trying to appear like something we are not. Our real need is to be who we are.

When the second seal is opened John sees a red horse whose rider carries a sword and takes peace from the earth. This is paralleled in Matthew 24:6-7 wear Jesus speaks of "wars and rumors of wars." For us this can depict the inner and outer "wars" we have that rob us of our peace. What we need is "the peace of God, which passes all understanding" (Philippians 4:7).

The opening of the third seal brings a black horse with its rider carrying a pair of scales. And John hears a voice saying, "A quart of wheat for a day's pay, and three quarts of barley for a day's pay." To me this is a pictorial representation of the famines spoken about in Matthew 24:7. Famine means that food is scarce, and when we apply this to what is going on inside us it speaks of not being fed spiritually—worse yet, being hungry emotionally. Remember Jesus said that we don't live be bread alone? We need food for our souls.

When the fourth seal is opened John sees a pale green horse whose rider is called, "Death" and Hades follows him. To me this is a pictorial representation of the pestilences spoken of by Jesus also in Matthew 24:7. This seal speaks of literal deaths, whereas we all experience inner deaths—as in the deaths we experience when we are rejected, abandoned, or betrayed. When we experience these things we suffer grief often as real as the grief we go through when we lose a loved one. And we have to work through these too. With this horseman our night-"mares" pass. But there are still three more seals to be opened.

When the fifth seal is opened John sees an altar, and under it are the souls of those who had been killed for the word of God. And they cried out with a loud voice, "How long O Lord till you avenge our blood?" And they are given the answer, not until their number is complete. A certain number must die first? Why? This shows that following Christ and doing what you are supposed to do doesn't assure you a smooth road ahead. Suffering is a reality, and according to the Buddha that is the First Nobel Truth. For a number of years I wore a crucifix even though I wasn't Catholic. I wore it because every time things were not going well, it reminded me that even Jesus suffered—so who was I to think that I should be spared suffering. This seal parallels what Jesus says in Matthew 24:9—"they will hand you over to be tortured and will put you to death . . ."

When the sixth seal is opened John sees a great earthquake, and he says that the sun became black, and the full moon became like blood—and the stars of the sky fell to the earth. And it says that everyone, slave and free hid in the caves and among the rocks of the mountains, calling to the mountains and rocks, "Fall upon us and hide us from the face of the one seated on the throne and from the wrath of the Lamb." The wrath of the Lamb? What's with that? To me the problem of suffering in the book of Revelation seems to be resolved by revenge. In the last seal the martyrs cry out, "How long O Lord till you avenge our blood?" Avenge has to do with revenge. And in the book of Revelation Jesus is not the embodiment of love, rather he is a sacrificial lamb with seven horns (5:6) and horns are made for goring—he is also depicted as the one who wears a robe dipped in blood and who leads the armies of heaven (19:13-14). And we read not only of the armies of heaven, but of war in heaven itself (12:7). Doesn't this seem a bit militant? But I guess this goes along with what it says in Ecclesiastes 3 —that there is a time to kill and a time to heal, and a time for war and a time for peace. But if there can also be war in heaven, then where will there be peace—or when? This seal parallels what Jesus says in Matthew 24:7, 29 about earthquakes and the sun, moon and stars.

When the Lamb opens the seventh seal we are told that there was silence in heaven for about a half an hour. Well thank God for that! I was wondering when we were going to have some silence. But I guess it's not for us after all, that is if we're still here on earth, because the silence is in heaven. But we all need times of silence in our lives, especially in the hectic world we live in. And here is a strange point (as if all of them in the book of Revelation weren't)—there is a whole chapter of other material between the sixth and the seventh seal. In studies of the Apocalypse chapter seven (which comes between the sixth and seventh seal) is called an "interlude." And so next we will look at the interlude.

CHAPTER 6

The 144,000 and the Great Multitude

THE 144,000 AND THE GREAT MULTITUDE

As I said earlier, chapter seven in the book of Revelation is an interlude between the sixth and seventh seals. It depicts two groups of people in a dramatic way as you will see.

After seeing what unfolded in the sixth seal, John sees four angels standing on the four corners of the earth, holding back the four winds so that the winds could not blow against the earth, sea or against any tree. Then he sees another angel ascending from the rising of the sun, having the seal of the living God. He hears this angel call out to the other four angels telling them not to allow the earth, sea or trees be damaged *until* the servants of God are marked with a seal on their foreheads. He hears the number of those sealed and it is 144,000 from the tribes of Israel—12,000 from each of the twelve tribes. When however you compare the twelve tribes that are named, you find that Dan and Ephraim are left out, and Levi and Joseph are added in their places. Some think the reason for this is because of a tradition that Dan and Ephraim were idolaters. There is no explanation given here however.

Next John sees "a great multitude" that no one could number, from every nation, kindred, people and tongue. They stand before the throne and the Lamb, robed in white and with palm branches in their hands. Interestingly enough the word for palm branches in the Greek is the same from which we get the word "phoenix." As the mythical bird, phoenix rose from the flames, so do these rise from "great tribulation," for when John enquires who these people are he is told, "These are they who have come out of great tribulation—they have washed their robes, and made them white in the blood of the Lamb." We are told that they will hunger and thirst no more, that the sun and heat will no longer scorch them, that they will be led to springs of living water, and that God will wipe away all tears from their eyes. Again in the book of Revelation being a Christian does not protect you from harm in fact over and over again we are told that the people of God must suffer here on earth. Our only consolation is in knowing that "there's a better home awaiting in the sky Lord, in the sky."

Just as I shared earlier that I believe that the twenty-four elders are made up of the twelve patriarchs of the twelve tribes of Israel, and the twelve apostles, so here I believe that we are seeing God's people being made up of both Jews and Gentiles. Throughout the Bible we are told that God would save a remnant of the Jews. This is a major concern for St. Paul in Romans 9-11. And here we see a remnant of each tribe of Israel "sealed" and a great multitude of Gentiles saved.

With that we conclude the interlude and move into what I feel is the most difficult part of the book of Revelation to interpret. Here I refer to what is known as the Seven Trumpets.

CHAPTER 7

The Seven Trumpets

THE SEVEN TRUMPETS

Chapter eight of the book of Revelation begins with the opening of the seventh seal, which brings silence to heaven for a half hour as was mentioned earlier. Then we begin with the seven trumpets which runs through chapters eight and nine, then there is another interlude between the sixth and the seventh trumpet which runs from verse one of chapter ten to verse thirteen of chapter eleven.

John sees seven more angels, who are given seven trumpets. Then John sees another angel who stands at the altar (there is an altar in heaven? More on that later) . . . This angel holds a golden censer filled with incense to be offered up with the prayers of the saints—its smoke rises before God. Then the angel fills the censer with fire from the altar and throws it to the earth—there are voices, thunder and lightning, and an earthquake. Now the seven angels make ready to blow their trumpets.

When the first angel blows his trumpet hail and fire mixed with blood are hurled onto the earth, and a third of the earth and trees are burned up, as well as all of the green grass. So much for ecology and being good stewards of the earth. It looks like we don't have to worry about global warming and burning the rainforests, it looks like God is going to turn up the heat and burn up the world for us.

When the second angel blows his trumpet—notice: "his" trumpet. No female angels are ever mentioned in the Bible. I guess heaven is a good ole' boys club, just like the male chauvinist ones down here on earth. Anyway, when the second angel blows his trumpet something like a great mountain burning with fire is thrown into the sea—"Baby I'm yours and I'll be yours until the mountain crumbles to the sea . . ." A third of the sea becomes blood, and a third of the living creatures in the sea are killed, and a third of the ships are destroyed. Watch out! Its God's reign of terror, and He's—notice the "He's again—this time He's giving us a break—He's only destroying a "third" of the sea—not all of it—at least not yet. We'll consider the significance of a "third" when we get to the Seven Last Plagues . . .

When the third angel blows his trumpet a great star fell from heaven. It falls on a third of the rivers and on the springs of water. There goes the thirds again. But a star? The sun is a star, and if it or any other star fell to earth the earth would be no more. John didn't know this, living thousands of years ago—before the Enlightenment. It would make sense if it was a meteor, but you would think that God knew what it was that fell to earth—or maybe He was just playing along with what John knew—for now we'll give Him the benefit of the doubt. The star has a name, and it is "Wormwood" and a third of the water became wormwood and many died from the water. The Greek word from which wormwood comes is the same root that our word, "absinthe" comes from. Absinthe was a drink that Vincent van Gogh among others drank, and which is illegal in the United States.

When the fourth angel blows his trumpet a third of the light of the sun, moon and stars is darkened. Then John sees an angel flying in the midst of heaven, saying with a loud voice, "Woe, woe, woe, to the inhabitants of the earth at the sounding of the trumpets that the three angels are about to blow."

When the fifth angel blows his trumpet John sees a star that had fallen from heaven to the earth and he was given the key to the bottomless pit. When he opens the bottomless pit smoke as from a great furnace comes out and the sun and air are darkened by the smoke. And there came out of the smoke scorpion-like locusts. Now here is where it gets really tricky—that is with trying to interpret. I said that as far as I am concerned the trumpets are the hardest things to interpret in the book of Revelation. But the fifth and sixth trumpets are the hardest of anything to interpret! We're told that the locusts were not to damage any grass or green growth or any trees, but only those who do not have the seal of God on their foreheads. These they were allowed to torture for five months.

Five months? When I was in seminary I wrote a major paper on the book of Revelation titled, "The Theological Use of Time in the Apocalypse." In the paper I dealt with the various time periods mentioned in the book and how they were dealt with by different schools of interpretation. Take for example what is known as the "Year/day principle." According to this school of interpretation a day equals a year in prophetic texts.[16] Therefore they would interpret the five months to be 150 years, because they understand a month to be thirty days times five and that comes to 150. And then they would try to hang a 150 year time period on

---

[16] They see precedence for this in texts such as Numbers14:33-34 and Ezekiel 4:6.

something in history. Others would interpret the five months to be five literal months that people would be tormented in the end times. And others see the five months to refer to the average lifespan of locusts. What do I think it means? Who knows? It's all just apocalyptic jibber jabber.

And we're told that when the locusts torture those who are unsealed, their torture is like scorpions. "And in those days people will seek death but will not find it—they will long to die, but death will flee from them" (verse 6). Wow! They will wish they could die! Remember 1 John 4:8 where it says, "God is love"? Is this "tough love" or is it "divine sadism"?

Then the text describes the locusts—it says they are like horses prepared for battle. They have crowns of gold, faces like human faces, hair like women, teeth like lions, scales like iron breastplates, tails like scorpions and the sound of their wings sounds like chariots rushing into battle! And it says that they have a king over them—the angel of the bottomless pit—named in the Hebrew, Abaddon (or Destruction) and in the Greek Apollyon (or Destroyer). Wow! These are some locusts! But what are they? I saw one futurist who said they were ancient descriptions of modern day attack helicopters. During the sixties I heard one evangelist say that they described bad acid trips. Some historicists see them as the Muslims spreading across Asia Minor, and Preterists see them as caricatures of the Parthians whom the Romans feared. Futurist see them in the future, Historicists see them in the somewhat distant past, Preterists see them in the first two centuries, and those who interpret them as being purely symbolic see them as always here—as the demons that haunt our inner lives. They are truly nightmare images.

This is the first "woe." There are still two more to come.

When the sixth angel blows his trumpet John hears a voice from the four horns of the golden altar before God, saying to the sixth angel, "Release the four angels who are bound at the great river Euphrates. When the four angels are loosed, who had been held ready for an hour, and a day, and a month, and a year—I'm surprised that they didn't get a week in there too—and a minute and a second. According to the year/day principle this would be 391 years + whatever an hour would be in relation to a year???

We are told that an army of two hundred million wearing breastplates the color of fire and of sapphire and of sulfur (which some futurists say could only be China) ride bizarre horses and kill a third of humanity. I said, "bizarre horses" because it says that their heads were like lions' heads, and fire, smoke and sulfur came out of their mouths, and the power of the horses is in their mouths and tails, and their tails are like serpents, having heads. These are truly night-"mares."

Then we are told that the other two-thirds of humanity who were not killed did not repent of their murders or fornication or thefts, nor did they give up worshiping demons and idols. So you know what's going to happen to them later . . .

When the seventh angel blows his trumpet John hears loud voices from heaven saying, "The kingdoms of the world have become the kingdom of our Lord, and His Christ, and he shall reign for ever and ever." Then the twenty-four elders fall on their faces and say (among other things) "We give you thanks, Lord God Almighty, who is, and was, and is to come for you have taken great power and begun to reign." They also thank God for "destroying those who destroy the earth." Now at first that sounds like an ecological statement, but on second thought it brings up the problem that in the book of Revelation it is God through his angels and minions who are the ones who are destroying the earth.

Then the seventh trumpet ends with the temple of God in heaven opened, and the ark of the covenant is seen. And there are flashes of lightening, and thunder, and an earthquake and great hail. Notice, we saw in the introduction to the seven trumpets that it said there is an altar in heaven. And here it says that the ark of the covenant is also in heaven. When we look at the book of Hebrews, especially chapters eight and nine we find that it talks about a "heavenly sanctuary." In fact it says that the earthly sanctuary which was built in the time of Moses was a shadow of the heavenly sanctuary. And Moses was told of God to, "See that you make everything according to the pattern that was shown you on the mountain" (Hebrews 8:5).

There is another interlude between the sixth and the seventh trumpet which runs from verse one of chapter ten to verse thirteen of chapter eleven. And so next we will look at the interlude.

CHAPTER 8

The Little Scroll and the Two Witnesses

THE LITTLE SCROLL AND THE TWO WITNESSES

In this chapter we're going to look at the interlude that comes between the sixth and seventh trumpets. The contents of this interlude takes up all of chapter ten and most of chapter eleven. Here we will first look at chapter ten which tells us of the "little scroll," then we will look at chapter eleven which tells us of the "two witnesses."

In chapter ten John sees another mighty angel coming down from heaven, wrapped in a cloud, with a rainbow over his head; his face like the sun, and his legs like pillars of fire. He holds a little scroll open in his hand. Notice: an "angel coming down from heaven." Heaven is "up there" and we're "down here." This makes no sense given what we know today. If the angel was coming down from heaven, where is heaven? Think of it—if you go up, you'll just keep going up. You'll pass planets and stars on the way out of the Milky Way galaxy and then out into open space and from there into a virtual infinity of "up there"—and you will never reach heaven. My own thought is that heaven is not "up there" but rather "in here." As Jesus says in Luke 17:20-21 ". . . the Kingdom of God does not come with observation. Neither shall they say, 'look here!' nor 'look there!' for the kingdom of God is within you."

The angel stands with his right foot on the sea and his left foot on the land and he gives a great shout like the roaring of a lion. When he shouts "the seven thunders" sound. When John is about to write, he hears a voice from heaven say, "Seal up what the seven thunders have said, and do not write it down." Why have the seven thunders spoken if you can't know what they said? Then the angel that is standing on the sea and the land raises his right hand to heaven and swears by him who lives forever and ever that there shall be no more delay. In the days when the seventh angel blows his trumpet the mystery of God will be fulfilled. The mystery of God is truly a mystery. We've already looked ahead at the seventh trumpet and besides voices from heaven saying that the kingdoms of this world have become the kingdom of the Lord, and God receiving the praises of the twenty-four elders, and the temple of God being opened in heaven with a view of the ark of the covenant, I don't see the mystery of God being fulfilled.

Next John hears the voice from heaven say, "Go take the scroll that is open in the hand of the angel who is standing on the sea and on the land"—so he does it. Then the voice tells him to eat the scroll and it is sweet as honey in his mouth, but bitter in his stomach. Now this is a play on something that happened to the prophet Ezekiel in the second and third chapters of his book. Eating a scroll symbolizes taking the word of God into one's self. And while the word is sweet in John's mouth, it ends up making him sick. And a good share of the message of the book of Revelation is pretty sickening.

And now on to chapter eleven and the two witnesses. Chapter eleven begins with John being given a measuring rod, and he is told to measure the temple of God, the altar, and those who worship there. But he is told not to measure the court outside the temple, for it has been given over to the nations to trample over it and the holy city for forty-two months. Then he is told that God's two witnesses will prophesy for one thousand two hundred sixty days wearing sackcloth.

Now here's another thing about the use of time in the book of Revelation. Forty-two months is twelve hundred and sixty days (30 x 42 = 1,260). It is also three and a half days. Because according to the year/ day principle a day in prophecy equals one year, so three times 360 = 1080 + 180 = 1,260. And what is the significance of this time period? Your guess is good as mine. Seventh-day Adventists who are historicists and sticklers over the year/day principle say that the 1,260 day period marks the time of papal supremacy which they believe was from 538 C.E. to 1798. Others think it is half of the prophetic week in Daniel 9:27. Some see it as a reference to the three and a half year drought in Elijah's time.[17] And still others think it is a reference to the three and a half year ministry of Jesus. To tell you the truth I don't think it's vital to our "salvation" (Oh, I hate to use that word!) to know for sure which one or another it is. But here's something else . . . the whole measuring thing is also a reference to Ezekiel's measuring which runs through Ezekiel 40-48. But what's the point? Who cares?

And then we come to the two witnesses who we are told in verse four of chapter eleven, are "the two olive trees and the two lampstands that stand before the Lord of the earth." This is taken right out of the fourth chapter of Zechariah. My Adventist friends say that the two witnesses are the Old and New Testaments. That however is a bit anachronistic

---

17   See: 1 King 18:1, Luke 4:25 and James 5:17.

because the New Testament did not even exist when John wrote the Apocalypse. I believe that once again they represent Israel and the followers of the lamb from every nation, kindred and tongue, as the twenty four elders for me represent the twelve patriarchs of the tribes of Israel, and the twelve apostles.

First we are told that if anyone tries to harm them, fire comes out of their mouths and destroys their enemies. But then later we are told that "the beast that comes out of the abyss" kills them. This is our first reference to the Beast. It says that the two witnesses prophesy for twelve hundred and sixty days and that they have authority over the springs of water—to turn them into blood, and they have authority to strike the earth with every kind of plague. When the beast kills them it says that their bodies will lie in the street for three and a half days in the great city where their Lord was crucified—which is symbolically named Sodom and Egypt—the first being destroyed by fire, and the second being destroyed by ten plagues. The people will rejoice at their deaths, but after three and a half days they are raised from the dead and fear falls on all who see. Then a voice from heaven says, "Come up here" and they ascend up to heaven in a cloud, as Christ did as we are told in the first chapter of Acts of the Apostles. And that same hour there is a great earthquake—so great that a tenth of the city falls, and seven thousand are killed. Then we are told that with this the second woe is past—so maybe this wasn't an interlude after all—if not the sixth trumpet is certainly the longest. Next, the third woe comes with the blowing of the seventh trumpet which we have already discussed in the last chapter.

CHAPTER 9

The Woman Clothed with the Sun

THE WOMAN CLOTHED
WITH THE SUN

Chapter twelve is for me the center of the book of Revelation. It reads like a great myth, and indeed some have compared it to the Greek myth of the birth of Apollo—but more on that later.

As the chapter opens, John sees a great wonder in heaven. A woman clothed with the sun, with the moon under her feet, and upon her head a crown with twelve stars. The woman is pregnant and she cries out in her birth pangs to be delivered.

But then another wonder appears in heaven—a great red dragon, having seven heads and ten horns, with crowns upon his heads. The dragon's tail drew a third of the stars of heaven and cast them to the earth. And he stood before the woman who was ready to deliver, to devour her child as soon as it was born.

The woman gives birth to a son, who is to rule all nations with a rod of iron. And her son is caught up to God and his throne. The woman flees into the wilderness where God prepared a place for her where she stays for one thousand two hundred sixty days (there's that number again!).

As I mentioned earlier, some have seen this as similar to the myth of the birth of Apollo by the goddess Leto.[18] The great dragon Python pursued Leto because he learned that she would bear a child who would kill him. Leto was carried off by the god Poseidon, who placed her on a remote island and then sank the island beneath the sea to hide her. After a vain search, Python went away to Parnassus, and Leto's island was brought back up. When the infant Apollo is born, he immediately gains full strength and he goes and slays Python on Mt. Parnassus.

There are also similarities to the Babylonian myth of the war between Tiamat, the seven-headed sea monster and the gods of heaven. In the war with Tiamat, a third of the stars are cast down from the heavens. So much for the uniqueness of scripture!

Of course the woman is Mary/the people of God, the dragon is the devil, and the son is none other than Christ.

Next we are told that there is a war in heaven. Michael and his angels fight the dragon and his

---

[18] See: Ben Witherington III's *Revelation*. Cambridge University Press.

angels. But the dragon and his angels are defeated and thrown out of heaven to the earth. And if you didn't guess it already John tells us that the great dragon was "that old serpent, called the Devil and Satan." We are told that the devil has come down to earth with great wrath for he knows that his time is short. Now I want to clarify a couple of things. The first is that this is the first time that the "old serpent"—presumably from the Garden of Eden is ever linked with the Devil or Satan. It never makes that connection in Genesis. We read about Satan in the opening of the book of Job, but again there is no connection with the serpent. It is only in the book of Revelation that this connection is made. And this is where my second point comes in. If the serpent was in reality Satan then his fall from heaven would have had to come before Eden. And yet the chronology of this chapter has the war in heaven, and Satan's expulsion from heaven happening after Christ ascends to heaven. I personally don't agree with this connection, and Eden and the serpent, and the devil and the war in heaven are both just myths—but they're not myths to live by. They are just myths like those of Leto, Apollo and Python, or Tiamat and her war in heaven. They're colorful but not true—at least not to me.

Next we find that when the dragon finds himself on the earth (again *after* the woman gives birth to the child and *not* before Eden) he pursues the woman. But the woman is given two wings like an eagle, and she flies to a place in the wilderness where she is nourished for "a time, and times, and half a time." Now here we go again. Remember how forty-two months = twelve hundred and sixty days? And how three and a half days also makes twelve hundred and sixty days—because according to the year/day principle a day in prophecy equals one year, so three times 360 = 1080 + 180 = 1,260. So a time (one day), times (two days), and half a time (half a day) equals three and a half days or years.

We are then told that the serpent (notice how he goes back and forth between calling it a dragon and serpent?) pours out a flood from his mouth to carry the woman away, but the earth helps the woman and swallows up the flood.

The chapter ends saying that the dragon was furious with the woman and went off to make war with the rest of her children—who keep the commandments of God and have the testimony of Jesus. For me these two things refer to John's concern for both the Jews and the Gentiles. Remember how I said that I believe the twenty four elders are made up of the twelve patriarchs of the tribes of Israel, and the twelve apostles? And how in chapter seven it showed us the two groups of the saved—the 144,000 of the tribes of Israel and the great multitude of every nation, kindred, people and tongue? Well here the commandments of God were given to the Jews in what is for us the Old Testament, and the Gentiles were given the testimony of Jesus.

Get ready, for in the next chapter we will meet the Beast!

CHAPTER 10

The Beast and His Mark

THE BEAST AND HIS MARK

And now we have come to the thirteenth chapter of the book of Revelation. Some people think that the number thirteen is unlucky. Well that certainly is the case in the Apocalypse (remember the Apocalypse is another name for the book of Revelation). It is here that we find the Beast, "the mark of the beast," and the dreaded number, 666. So let's dig in!

The chapter begins with John seeing a beast rise up out of the sea. It has seven heads and ten horns, and upon his horns ten crowns (sound familiar?), and upon this heads the name of blasphemy. Remember the great red dragon had seven heads and ten horns, but he had seven crowns on his heads, and the beast has ten crowns on his horns. It's probably pointless to speculate as to the significance of these differences.

And whereas the dragon had the body of a dragon, the beast looks like a leopard, with the feet of a bear, and the mouth of a lion. And we are told that the dragon (who is you know who) gives the beast great power and authority. But you might have noticed by now that John takes much of his imagery from the Hebrew Bible. And this is no exception, for here he constructs his beast from a prophecy in the seventh chapter of the book of Daniel. But before we get to Daniel I've got to come clean on something. I'm sure if you are a conservative Christian you most certainly believe that God gave John these visions, and he passively received them. Theologians talk of different theories of inspiration. Most conservative Christians believe in what is referred to as "Verbal Inspiration." This view holds that God says to the Bible writer exactly what he wants them to write down, and the Bible writer writes down word for word what God says like a secretary taking down dictation. Those who hold this view believe that the Bible is verbally inspired—word for word. Given this, they would believe that John is just passively writing down what God wants him to write, and that he also is writing down descriptions of what God is showing him in vision. Therefore John does not "construct" what he writes using various passages from the prophetic works of the Hebrew Bible and then just say that he was shown these things in vision. No they believe that God gave John all these things and he just wrote them down. I on the other hand believe that John constructed his book by adapting the various prophetic works of the Hebrew

Bible for his own purpose—which was to show that though the early Christians were suffering from the persecution of the Romans as well as from those who said they were Jews but are not, rather they are "the synagogue of Satan"—though they were being persecuted God would soon avenge their blood, and their persecutors would get their just rewards. I point out again that God is not love in the book of Revelation as it says in 1 John 4:8—and by the way, it wasn't the same John who wrote the book of Revelation. The author of Revelation was not the same John who wrote the gospel of John or the epistles of John. So if I didn't succeed in popping your theological bubble, you probably think that I will probably meet my end along with the Romans and the synagogue of Satan.

Anyway, back to the beast. As you remember, I was just about ready to take you to the seventh chapter of the book of Daniel. There we find some of the material that John lifted from Daniel. We are told that during the first year of the reign of Belshazzar, King of Babylon, Daniel had a dream. He dreamt that he saw four beasts coming up from the sea (remember the beast in Revelation also came up out of the sea?). The first is like a lion with eagle's wings, the second was like a bear, the third was like a leopard with four heads and four wings, and the fourth was dreadful and terrible and had ten horns.

And what did the beast in Revelation look like? It is actually a combination of the four beasts in Daniel. It too was dreadful and had ten horns, and it has a body like a leopard, the feet of a bear, and the mouth of a lion. So, all four beasts are incorporated into John's beast. I think what he is saying given this is that the beast that the Christians were facing in John's time was worse than all of the other four beasts combined.

Then John says that he sees that one of this beast's heads had a deadly wound, but the wound was healed and the entire world wondered after the beast. The Protestant reformers thought that the beast was the papacy. And many historicists today still believe that the beast was and is the papacy. Futurists on the other had have seen the beast as Hitler and the Nazis, Communism in general and Stalin in specific (and Mikhail Gorbachev even had a mark on his head!), Saddam Hussein (who had Babylon, and the Euphrates going for him) and who will be the next candidate for the beast? Who knows?

And then it says that the people worship the dragon who gives power to the beast. It also says that it was given a mouth which speaks great things and blasphemies, and power is given it to continue for forty two months—there we go again! John is really stuck on this forty two month thing!

We are told that the beast is allowed to make war with the saints (or people of God, not like St. Francis) and to overcome them. And power was given to him over all kindred, tongues and nations. You've got to be kidding me! God is allowing this to happen? Not only is God allowing the beast to make war with the saints, God is allowing the beast to overcome them? What does this tell you about God? Would you allow someone to beat up your kids? Would that be the loving thing to do? But then again, we're not God . . .

It says that those whose names are not written in the book of life will worship the beast—the book of life of "the Lamb slain from the foundation of the world."

We then read something of the ethics of the book of Revelation. "He that kills with the sword must be killed with the sword." Lex talionis—the law of retaliation—"an eye for an eye, a tooth for a tooth." This is Old Testament ethics at its worst. And after saying, "He that kills with the sword must be killed with the sword" it says, "Here is the patience and the faith of the saints." Be patient, I'll see that they're all killed. I will avenge your blood—that I allowed them to bloody you in the first place.

Then John sees another beast which rises out of the earth. He has two horns like a lamb, but speaks like a dragon. This is a beast in sheep's clothing! He exercises all the power of the first beast, and causes all on earth to worship the first beast. This beast also performs great signs—making fire come down from heaven, and he deceives them on earth by means of the miracles which he has power to do. And he says that they should make an image to the first beast. And he has power to give life to the image of the beast, that it should speak, and causes all who will not worship the image of the beast to be killed.

The beast with lamb-like horns also causes all, both small and great, rich and poor, free and slave to receive a mark on their right hand or forehead—and that no one can buy or sell who does not have the mark, or the name of the beast, or the number of his name. Then it gives us this clue: "Let anyone with understanding count the number of the beast, for it is the number of a man and his number is 666." There has been much speculation as to what the mark of the beast is. I have heard Seventh-day Adventists say that the mark is Sunday observance. And in the hippy era I heard a preacher say that it was the "peace sign." Many futurists say that it is bar codes or some kind of chip that is implanted in the hand that can be scanned instead of a credit card. They speak of a moneyless society. However I can't imagine them putting a chip in your forehead. But what most preterists believe is that it is a reference to the Roman Emperor, Nero, because Nero Caesar in Hebrew adds up to 666.

CHAPTER 11

The 144,000 and the Three Angel's Messages

THE 144,000 AND THE THREE ANGELS' MESSAGES

In chapter fourteen we meet the 144,000 again. This time they are standing with the Lamb on Mt. Zion, and his Father's name is written on their foreheads. John hears a voice from heaven that seems hard to describe because he says that it is like the sound of many waters, like the sound of loud thunder, and like the sound of harpist playing their harps—harps that sound like thunder? And it says that the 144,000 sing a new song before the throne and the living creatures and the elders. And no one could learn that song except the 144,000. They have not defiled themselves with women, for they are virgins. Now I've got to stop here for a moment. No one can sing their song, because no one has gone through what they have gone through. But the "defiling themselves with women" is definitely not to be taken literally. I don't know about you, but I don't believe that women defile men. The whole idea of women literally defiling comes from Old Testament times and especially from the book of Leviticus chapter twelve and fifteen where it speaks of women as ceremonially unclean after they give birth to a child, and whenever they bleed. I think that this is pure bull shit! Taken figuratively what this means is that the 144,000 which are the remnant of the Jews have never worshipped other gods, unlike the Gentiles. In the book of Revelation we find two women: the woman clothed with the sun, who represented Mary and the people of God in general, and the woman clothed in purple and scarlet in chapter seventeen who is referred to as "the great whore" and who we will find out later represents Rome which persecuted the people of God.[19]

We are also told that the 144,000 are the first fruits of the redeemed, and that they follow the Lamb wherever he goes.

Then we come to the three angels' messages. We're told that the first angel is flying midheaven, with the everlasting gospel to proclaim to them who dwell on the earth. He says with a loud voice,

---

[19] In the Hebrew Bible the people of God are seen as the bride of God, and worshipping other gods is seen as adultery and unfaithfulness. See: Ezekiel 16 & 23, and Hosea.

"Fear God, and give glory to him; for the hour of his judgment has come, and worship him who made heaven, and earth, and the sea, and the springs of water." Often times I have heard preachers say that "Fear God" should really be "Respect God" because we should not be afraid of God. These preachers must have never read the book of Revelation, because here God is someone to be feared. Then it says, "the hour of his judgment has come"—that is in John's present, not in the distant future. And this is because John believed he was living in the end times. Revelation begins in the first verse of the entire book by saying that this is the Revelation of "things which must *shortly* come to pass." Then in the third verse it says, "Blessed are those who read, and they who hear the words of this prophecy, and keep those things which are written therein, for the time is *near.*" And then in the closing chapter it says, "See, I am coming *soon*" (verse 7), "See, I am coming *soon*" (verse 12), and "Surely I am coming *soon*" (verse 20). So John believed he was living in the last days, and the hour of God's judgment had come.

Then the second angel followed saying, "Babylon is fallen, is fallen, that great city, because she made all nations drink of the wine of the wrath of her fornication." Babylon in code is Rome as we shall see when we come to the seventeenth chapter. And so the announcement of the fall of Babylon is really the announcement of the fall of Rome. It might seem like Rome has the upper hand on the Christians, but soon Rome will fall.

And then when we come to the third angel we hear a truly fearful message, for the third angel says with a loud voice, "If anyone worships the beast and his image, and receives his mark on their forehead, or on their hand, they will also drink the wine of God's wrath, poured unmixed into the cup of his indignation, and they shall be tormented with fire and brimstone in the presence of the holy angels, and in the presence of the Lamb. And the smoke of their torment goes up forever and ever, and they have no rest day or night, those who worship the beast and his image, and whoever receives the mark of his name."

And so "Fear God" really means "be afraid, be very afraid." This is real "fire and brimstone" but it's not all out hell yet. We'll come to that when we get to chapter twenty.

. Then it says, "Here is the patience of the saints"—just wait and they'll get theirs. And it tells us that the saints are those who keep the commandments of God, and the faith of Jesus. And again I point out the two groups of the saved in the book of Revelation: the commandments = the Jews, and the faith of Jesus = the Gentiles. In reality all of God's people keep the commandments, but this is just shorthand to say that the Gentiles who believe in Jesus will be joined by the promised remnant of the Jews.

Then John says he hears a voice from heaven say, "Write, blessed are the dead who die in the Lord from henceforth. Yes, the Spirit says, they shall rest from their labors, and their works follow them."

Next John sees a white cloud, and upon the cloud sits one like the Son of Man, having on his head a crown, and in his hand a sharp sickle. Another angel comes out of the temple and cries out to the one on the cloud, "Thrust in your sickle, and reap, for the time has come to reap, and the harvest of the earth is ripe." And so he reaps. Then another angel comes out of the temple in heaven also having a sharp sickle. An angel then comes out from the altar who has power over fire and tells the angel with the sickle to thrust in his sickle and gather the grapes that are now ripe. So he does, and then casts the grapes into "the great winepress of the wrath of God." It seems that God has some real anger issues, and he acts it out too!

It then says that the winepress is trodden outside the city, and blood comes out of the winepress as high as a horse's bridle, and for a distance of about two hundred miles. Now that's a lot of blood. "He is trampling out the vintage where the grapes of wrath are stored . . . his truth is marching on." His truth???

CHAPTER 12

The Seven Last Plagues

THE SEVEN LAST PLAGUES

When we looked at the seven trumpets we saw that their destruction affected a "third" of whatever they were destroying. I said we would consider the significance of these thirds when we got to the seven last plagues. And here we are. Below I compare the ten plagues that fell on Egypt in the book of Exodus with the seven trumpets and the seven last plagues. And you'll see that there are some similarities between them. The significance of the thirds I see as a progression of destruction between the three series of plagues. So where as the plagues that fell on Egypt were local, the plagues that fall with the seven trumpets are enlarged to a third of the earth, and finally the plagues that fall with the seven last plagues are universal—affecting the whole earth.

Exodus 7-12	Revelation 8-11	Revelation 15-16
River turned to blood	Sea turned to blood	Sea turned to blood Rivers turned to blood
Frogs		Frogs
Gnats		
Flies		
Death of livestock	Horses	
Boils		Sores
Hail and fire	Hail and fire	Hail
Locusts	Locusts	
Darkness	Darkness	Darkness
Death of firstborn		

With that being said we will now move into chapters fifteen and sixteen where we will look more closely at the seven last plagues.

First John tells us that he saw another sign in heaven—great and marvelous. He saw seven angels having the seven last plagues, for with them the wrath of God is ended. And he also sees what looks to him like a sea of glass, and on it those who had gotten the victory over the beast—and they have harps. This is where they get the stereotype of heaven being a place where you sit on clouds and play harps. And it says that they sing the song of Moses and the song of the Lamb saying,

> Great and marvelous are your works,
> Lord God Almighty.
> Just and true are your ways,
> O king of the saints.
> Who shall not fear you, O Lord,
> And glorify your name?
> For only you are holy,
> For all nations shall come
> And worship before you
> For your judgments are made manifest.

After this he looked and saw that the temple in heaven was opened, and the seven angels came out of the temple, having the seven plagues. They were clothed in pure white linen, having their breasts girded with golden girdles. It seems strange to me to have the seven last plagues in the temple in heaven—the holiest place in the universe with the causes of death and destruction. But I guess plagues would be a holy thing if your God was the God of vengeance.

Then one of the four living creatures gave the seven angels seven golden bowls full of the wrath of God. And the temple was filled with smoke from the glory of God, and no one could enter the temple until the seven plagues were ended.

Then John hears a loud voice from the temple telling the seven angels to go and pour out their bowls of the wrath of God on the earth.

When the first angel pours out his bowl, a foul and painful sore came on those who had the mark of the beast.

The second angel pours out his bowl into the sea, and it becomes like blood, and every living thing in the sea dies.

The third angel pours out his bowl into the rivers and springs of water, and they become blood. And the third angel says, "You are just, O Holy One, for you have judged these—because they shed the blood of the saints and prophets, you have given them blood to drink. It is what they deserve!" And then John hears a voice from the altar say, "Yes, O Lord God Almighty, your judgments are true and just!"

When the fourth angel pours out his bowl on the sun, it is allowed to scorch people. But they curse God and do not repent and give him glory. You know, it seems that God is what we used to call, "A glory hog." It seems that God's self-esteem is such that he needs to be praised continually.

The fifth angel pours out his bowl on the throne of the beast, and his kingdom was plunged into darkness. The people gnawed their tongues in pain, and cursed God, and did not repent of their deeds.

The sixth angel pours out his bowl on the great river Euphrates and its waters are dried up in order to prepare the way for the kings of the east. And John sees three foul spirits like frogs coming out of the mouth of the dragon, out of the beast, and out of the false prophet. These are demonic spirits, performing signs—who go to the kings of the world to assemble them for battle on the great day of God. And they assemble them at a place that is called, Armageddon—as in the battle of Armageddon!

When the seventh angel pours out his bowl into the air, a loud voice comes out of the temple, from the throne saying, "It is done!" And there comes a violent earthquake. The great city is split into three parts, and the cities of the nations fell. God remembers (does he sometimes forget?) great Babylon and gives her the cup of the wine of the fierceness of his wrath. And every island fled away, and the mountains were not found. And there fell great hail out of heaven, every one being about a hundred pounds. And the people cursed God for the plague of hail.

CHAPTER 13

The Whore of Babylon

THE WHORE OF BABYLON

Chapter seventeen is a great chapter if you like whores, because it begins with the words, "Then one of the seven angels who had the seven bowls came and said, 'Come, I will show you the judgment of the great whore who is seated on many waters, with whom the kings of the earth have committed fornication, and with the wine of whose fornication the inhabitants of the earth have become drunk.'" Wow! We've got a whore and fornication, and we've got wine and drunkenness!

In the book of Revelation we have contrasting polarities. We have the New Jerusalem and Babylon, the seal of God and the mark of the beast, God and the dragon, the Lamb and the beast, the Holy Spirit and the false prophet, and the Woman clothed with the sun, and the whore of Babylon.

As I mentioned earlier, the woman clothed with the sun represented Mary/the people of God, while the whore of Babylon represents Rome which persecuted the people of God as we shall see in this chapter.

We read, "So he carried me away in the spirit into the wilderness, and I saw a woman sitting upon a scarlet colored beast, full of names of blasphemy, having seven heads and ten horns." We've already seen that both the dragon and the beast each have seven heads and ten horns, and so does the scarlet beast here. And it says that the woman is clothed in purple and scarlet, and is adorned in gold, precious stones and pearls, and holds a golden cup full of abominations and the filthiness of her fornication. And the woman is drunk with the blood of the saints.

Then an angel says to John that he will tell him the mystery of the woman and of the beast which carries her. He says that the beast was, and is not, and is about to ascend from the bottomless pit and go to destruction. And those whose names are not in the book of life will be amazed when they see the beast. Then he says that the seven heads are seven mountains upon which the woman is seated (Rome is the city on seven hills)—they are also seven kings, of whom five have fallen, one is living, and the other has not yet come, and when he comes, he must remain only a little while. As for the beast that was and is not, it is an eighth but belongs to the seven. Many see the seven kings as seven Roman Emperors during the first century of the Common Era.

As for the ten horns they are said to be ten kings who have not yet received a kingdom, but they are to receive authority as kings for "one hour" (a short time?) together with the beast. These all will make war with the Lamb, but the Lamb will defeat them because he is King of kings and Lord of lords.

Next we are told that the waters that you saw where the whore is seated are peoples and multitudes and nations and tongues. And the ten horns and the beast will hate the whore and will make her desolate—for "God has put it into their hearts to carry out his purpose by agreeing to give their kingdom to the beast, until the words of God will be fulfilled." God makes these kings the puppets of his purpose.

And in the end we are told that the woman, who is the great whore, is that great city that rules over the kings of the earth—she is Rome itself.

Then when we come to chapter eighteen we read of the fall of Babylon or Rome. First John sees another angel come down from heaven who cries with a loud voice, "Babylon the great is fallen, is fallen, and has become the habitation of devils, and the haunt of every foul spirit, and a haunt of every unclean and hateful bird." The angel goes on to say that all nations have drunk of the wine of the wrath of her fornication, and the kings of the earth have committed fornication with her, and the merchants of the earth have grown rich through the abundance of her delicacies.

Then he hears another voice from heaven saying, "Come out of her my people, that you be not partakers of her sins, and that you receive not of her plagues. For her sins have reached unto heaven, and God has remembered her iniquities." Then it says that she will be repaid double for what she has done. As she has glorified herself and lived in luxury, so she will be given a like measure of torment and sorrow. As she has said she is a queen, and no widow, and she will never see sorrow, therefore her plagues will come in one day—death, mourning, and famine—and she will be utterly burned with fire, for "strong is the Lord God who judges her."

The kings of the earth who committed fornication and lived in luxury with her will weep and wail over her when they see the smoke of her burning, and they will stand afar saying, "Alas, alas, the great city, Babylon, the mighty city! For in one hour her judgment has come." Above it said her plagues would come in one day. Now it says her judgment comes in one hour. Day, hour, whatever . . .

The we are told that the merchants of the earth will weep and mourn for her, since no one buys their cargo anymore—cargo of precious metals, jewels and pearls, precious fabrics, ivory and costly woods, incense, wine, olive oil, flour, cattle and sheep, horses and chariots, and slaves. And the merchants too will stand afar saying, "Alas, alas, that great city, clothed in linen, in purple and scarlet, adorned with gold, with jewels and pearls! For in one hour all this wealth has been laid waste!"

And all the shipmasters and seafarers who trade on the sea, will stand afar saying, "What city was like the great city?" And they throw dust on their heads and weep and mourn crying out, "Alas, alas, that great city, where all who had ships at sea grew rich by her wealth![20] For in one hour she has been laid waste."

Then it says that the people of God are to rejoice for God has given judgment for them against her. For and against—for us, against her.

Next John sees a mighty angel take up a stone like a great millstone, and cast it into the sea saying, "Thus with violence shall that great city Babylon be thrown down, and shall be found no more."[21]

Finally we are told that the sound of musicians will be heard no more in her, nor the sound of the craftsman will not be found in her, and the light of a candle will not shine anymore in her, and the voice of the bridegroom and of the bride will be heard no

---

[20]   Compare with Ezekiel 27:26-36.
[21]   See: Jeremiah 51:63-64.

more in her. Her merchants were the most powerful on earth, and with her false magic she deceived all the people of the world![22]

And the chapter closes with these words, "And in her was found the blood of prophets, and of saints, and of all that were slain upon the earth."

---

[22] See: Ezekiel 26:13-14.

CHAPTER 14

Two Suppers and the Rider on a White Horse

TWO SUPPERS AND THE RIDER ON A WHITE HORSE

Next John hears what seems to be the loud voice of a great multitude. They are saying, "Hallelujah . . . he has judged the great whore . . . and he has avenged on her the blood of his servants." Then they say Hallelujah again. Finally God is avenging for the "souls under the altar"—I guess the number of those who had to die is now complete (see: 6:9-11).

Then the twenty-four elders and the four living creatures fall down and worship God saying, "Amen. Hallelujah!"

And from the throne a voice says, "Praise our God, all you his servants, and all who fear him, small and great."

Then comes another "Hallelujah!" this time from a great multitude. And this time they announce the marriage of the Lamb for his "bride has made herself ready." And an angel says, "Blessed are those who are invited to the marriage supper of the Lamb." That's the first supper.

John then says that he sees heaven opened, and there is a white horse, and its rider is called Faithful and True, and in righteousness he judges and makes war. Somehow when I think of Jesus I just don't think of him making war. Remember he said, "Blessed are the peace makers." But here he is on a white horse with his eyes like flames of fire and a sharp sword coming out of his mouth with which to strike down the nations, and he will rule them with a rod of iron, and he is wearing a robe dipped in blood. And we're told that he will tread the wine press of the fury of the wrath of God. Fury? Wrath? No God is love here.

Now comes the second supper. John tells us that he sees an angel standing in the sun (apparently angels are fire resistant) and he calls to all the birds to "Come, gather for the great supper of God, to eat the flesh of kings, the flesh of captains, the flesh of the mighty, the flesh of horses and their riders—flesh of all, both free and slave, both small and great." Wow! That sounds like a tasty treat! I know, I'm such a wise ass.

Then John sees the beast and the kings of the earth with their armies gathered to make war against the rider on the horse and his army. But the beast and the false prophet are captured and thrown alive into the lake of fire. And the rest are killed with the sword that comes out of Christ's mouth, and the birds are "gorged with their flesh."

CHAPTER 15

The Millennium

.

THE MILLENNIUM

Though the word, "Millennium" never appears in the book of Revelation, chapter twenty is where it comes from because it is here that it speaks of a period of time that is a thousand years.

John sees and angel coming down from heaven (heaven is up there?) holding in his hand the key to the bottomless pit and a great chain. He seizes the dragon "that ancient serpent, who is the Devil and Satan" and binds him for a thousand years. The angel throws him into the bottomless pit and locks it and seals it over him so that he cannot deceive the nations until the thousand years are ended. And after that he will be let out for a little while—I wonder how little, is little?

Then John sees the souls of those who had been beheaded for not worshipping the beast come to life and they are given authority to judge, and they reign with Christ for the thousand years. "The rest of the dead did not come to life until the thousand years were ended. This is the first resurrection." Over these the second death has no power. It is these that judge those who are not resurrected.

When the thousand years are over Satan is released from his prison and he comes out to deceive the nations—they are as numerous as the sands of the sea. They march up over the breadth of the earth and surround the camp of the saints and the beloved city. But fire comes down from heaven and consumes them. And the devil is thrown into the lake of fire, where the beast and false prophet are, and they are tormented day and night forever and ever.

Then John sees a great white throne and the one who sits on it. And he sees the dead, great and small, standing before the throne. And the books are opened, and the book of life. And the dead are judged according to what they had done. He's making a list and checking it twice, He's going to find out who's naughty and nice. Is this salvation by works rather than substitutionary atonement? St. Paul makes it clear in his writings that people are not saved by their works, rather Christ died as our substitute so that we could be saved by his works instead of our own. But the book of Revelation does not agree with Paul. In fact it says that the bride of Christ has "been granted to be clothed with fine linen" but the fine linen is not the righteousness of Christ but rather "the righteous deeds of the saints" (19:8). And anyone whose name is not found in the book of life is thrown into the lake of fire.

CHAPTER 16

Heaven on Earth

HEAVEN ON EARTH

Have you ever heard of the "Pearly Gates?"—and about "walking on streets of gold?" Well, we've come to the two closing chapters of the book of Revelation where we will see the Pearly Gates and the streets of gold.

Notice that I have titled this chapter, "Heaven on Earth"? That's because whereas most people think of heaven as being "up there"—according to the book of Revelation, heaven will ultimately be down here. Here is how these closing chapters begin:

> "Then I saw a new heaven and a new earth—for the first heaven and the first earth had passed away and there was no more sea (what's the hang up with the sea?). And I saw the holy city, the New Jerusalem, coming down out of heaven from God, prepared as a bride adorned for her husband. And I heard a loud

voice from the throne saying, 'See, the home of God is now among mortals. God will dwell with them, and they shall be his people, and God himself shall be with them, and be their God.'"

As a line I once heard in a gospel song, "Heaven came down, and glory filled my soul." The holy city, the New Jerusalem comes down to earth, and God lives among us! Wow!

Next we are given these promises, which I quoted often in funerals and memorial services back in the days when I was still a practicing minister:

"And God shall wipe away all tears from their eyes, and there shall be no more death, neither sorrow, nor crying, neither shall there be any more pain, for the former things are passes away."

Then we hear the voice from the throne (I'm guessing its God) say, "See, I am making all things new" and he tells John to write down that these things are trustworthy and true. Then he says, "It is done!" It seems that at this point the whole experiment which was called the earth and humanity is done—finis—over.

The voice from the throne then let's us know whose talking, for he says, "I am Alpha and Omega, the beginning and the end. I will give to those who thirst the fountain of the water of life freely." Those who overcome ("We shall overcome . . .") will inherit these things, and I will be their God (there it is! The mysterious voice from the throne is God!) and they will be my children." But here comes the bad news . . . it's a laundry list of those who will end up in the lake of fire, rather than on this heaven on earth: the fearful, the unbelieving, the abominable (which I guess would include the Abominable Snowman), murderers, whoremongers, sorcerers, idolaters, and all liars. Remember, he's making a list, and checking it twice—so you better make sure that you're not involved in any of the things mentioned in the above list. I wonder if there is any "wiggle room" in any of this? What about "white lies?" And here's an interesting aside . . . the Greek word that is translated "sorcerers" is pharmakia which actually suggests drug use. So what kind of drugs if any, are okay? Will you end up in the lake of fire if you take antidepressants? Or blood pressure medication. Or does this just mean illegal drugs? But there are all kinds of drugs today that did not even exist at the time John wrote Revelation—like heroine for example, but then morphine would be okay if administered by a physician. And what about marijuana? In the first chapter of the Bible—Genesis 1:29 it says that God says, "See, I have given you every herb bearing seed that is upon the face of all the earth . . ." and God even says it is all very good. I like the herbs, but can people make laws against using what God has given us. And if you say it says that God gave it to us to eat, not to smoke. Well then, I'll eat it!

Then we're told that one of the angels who had the bowls of the seven last plagues, came to John and said, "Come, I will show you the bride, the wife of the Lamb." John says that the angel carried him away in the spirit to a high mountain and showed him the New Jerusalem coming down out of heaven from God. He says that it has a high wall (you'll see just how high in a moment) with twelve gates that are pearls, and you guessed it, the streets of the city are gold! On the twelve gates are inscribed the names of the twelve tribes of Israel. And the wall of the city has twelve foundations, and on them are the names of the twelve apostles. Here again is the theme that I have mentioned a number of times in this book. And that is the people of God are made up of followers of the lamb from every nation, kindred, and tongue, and a faithful remnant of the tribes of Israel. We first saw this in the twenty-four elders who I believe are made up of the patriarchs of the twelve tribes of Israel, and the twelve apostles. Then we saw in chapter seven the 144,000 from the tribes of Israel along side of the great multitude of every nation, kindred and tongue. Then we saw it in the "two witnesses" and then in those who keep the commandments of God (Jews) and those who hold the testimony of Jesus (those of every nation, kindred and tongue). And here finally we see it in the gates of the twelve tribes of Israel, and the foundations of the twelve apostles.

The city we are told lies four-square with its length, width and height the same. And they are each fifteen hundred miles! Fifteen hundred miles high? This is one high city! So the new earth must be a lot bigger to accommodate such a large city or else the planet would tip over under the great weight of the city. The wall is said to be nearly seventy-five yards high. And besides the great size of the city is the complete gaudiness of it, for if you read verses 18-21 of chapter 21 you'll find that it is decorated with all kinds of precious stones and gold.

John tells us that there is no temple in the city, for the temple is God himself and the Lamb. And the city has no need of the sun or moon, for the glory of God and the Lamb are its light. Its gates are never shut, and there will be no night there—so much for those who love the nightlife—but then again, "those kind of people" will probably be in the lake of fire anyway. Only those who are written in the Lamb's book of life will be there.

And now for the final chapter! Here John says that the angel showed him the river of the water of life which flows from the throne of God and the Lamb through the middle of the street of the city. On either side of the river is the tree of life which has twelve kinds of fruit, and produces its fruit each month. And the leaves of the tree are for the healing of the nations.

Then again John is told that "These words are trustworthy and true." It seems you need to hear this twice—you need some extra reinforcement to believe a story like this.

We're told that God has sent his angel "to show his servants what must soon take place." But how soon is soon? And this is even added to with the words, "See, I am coming soon!" Then he is told not to seal up the words of this prophecy "for the time is near." Then it is said again, "See, I am coming soon and my reward is with me, to repay everyone according to their works." Again "soon"—there is a real sense of urgency to this book, and yet it's been nearly two thousand years and it hasn't happened yet—unless I'm in purgatory right now and only believe I'm living a somewhat normal life on earth. And what about repaying us according to our works? This doesn't sound like salvation by faith in the substitutionary atonement in Christ—so much emphasized by good ole' St. Paul.

Then again we see the list of those who will not be allowed in the city but this time they add "dogs" along with the sorcerers, whoremongers, murderers, idolaters and liars. What's wrong with dogs? I thought that they were "man's best friend." And what's this about being outside the city? I thought they were in the lake of fire. So does this suggest that the lake of fire is on earth, outside the city? Who knows? As they say, "It's all Greek to me"—and it really is for me.

And then comes the altar call: "The Spirit and the bride say, 'Come.' And let everyone who hears say, 'Come.' And let everyone who is thirsty come. And whosoever will, let them take the water of life freely."

Then given the rest of the book, it couldn't end without one more curse:

"If anyone adds to the words of this prophecy, God will add to that person the plagues described in this book, and if anyone takes away from the words of this prophecy, God will take away that person's share in the tree of life and in the holy city, which are described in this book."

Jesus then says one final time, "Surely I am coming soon." And then there is a benediction: "The grace of the Lord Jesus be with all the saints. Amen."

POSTSCRIPT

POSTSCRIPT

Despite the way I have sometimes spoken about things in the book of Revelation I have had a great love for the book from my teen years on. In high school I would get up early in the morning before school and study the book of Revelation while I sipped on my coffee. Then while in my church youth group I would study the book of Revelation with my youth pastor. I have already mentioned that I wrote a major paper in seminary on the use of time in the book of Revelation. And finally, over the near thirty years of my ministry I have done many, many Revelation seminars—one of my last at the Sisters of Mercy convent here in Auburn where I live. So I think that you can see that I have had a great love for the book. But in studying it so closely over the years, I have also found a number of faults which I have described here.

Most students of the Apocalypse, given the curses in its last chapter would never think to be critical of the book. But I felt that I had to be honest, even if it means me receiving its curses. Someone had to do it, and I offered my self up for this sacrifice. Some readers will be appalled at what I have written here, but perhaps there will be a few that will take it with a light heart and even thank me for what I have done. Either way is alright with me, for I now say, "It is done!"

Printed in Great Britain
by Amazon